Collins

easy lea

Addition and subtraction

quick quizzes

Ages 5–7

Trevor Dixon

Counting on

Write the answers to the sums.

1 $3 + 2 = $ ☐

2 $4 + 4 = $ ☐

3 $3 + 4 = $ ☐

4 $7 + 1 = $ ☐

5 $3 + 5 = $ ☐

6 $2 + 4 = $ ☐

7 $5 + 5 = $ ☐

8 $5 + 4 = $ ☐

9 $7 + 6 = $ ☐

10 $6 + 4 = $ ☐

Count the pictures to help you add the numbers.

Colour your score

Taking away

Write the answers.

Cross out the number being subtracted and count what is left.

1    5 – 1 = ☐

2    4 – 2 = ☐

3    6 – 3 = ☐

4    7 – 4 = ☐

5  8 – 2 = ☐

6 9 – 4 = ☐

7  5 – 5 = ☐

8 7 – 0 = ☐

9 6 – 5 = ☐

10 9 – 3 = ☐

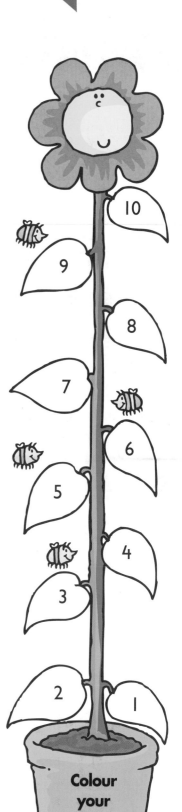

Colour your score

3

Number facts to 20

Write the answers.

Check the sign. There are some additions and some subtractions.

1 ◯◯ + ◯◯   = 2 + 2 = ☐

2 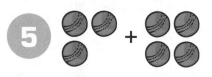 = 4 – 1 = ☐

3 = 1 + 4 = ☐

4 = 7 – 2 = ☐

5 = 3 + 4 = ☐

6 = 5 – 3 = ☐

7 = 2 + 6 = ☐

8 = 8 – 0 = ☐

9 = 7 + 8 = ☐

10 = 11 – 4 = ☐

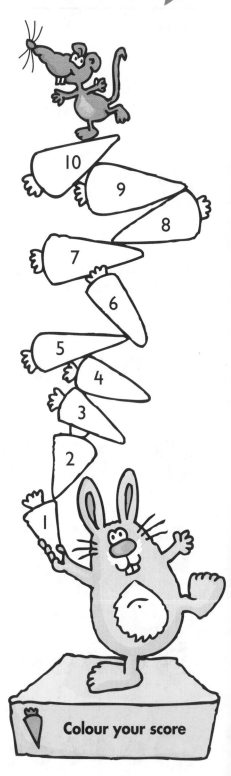

Colour your score

4

Addition

Write the answers to these sums.

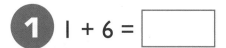

0   10   20

1   1 + 6 =

2   2 + 4 =

3   5 + 1 =

4   7 + 2 =

5   6 + 0 =

6   6 + 5 =

7   9 + 2 =

8   4 + 8 =

9   1 + 9 =

10   7 + 7 =

11   5 + 9 =

12   9 + 1 =

13   2 + 7 =

14   8 + 9 =

15   8 + 6 =

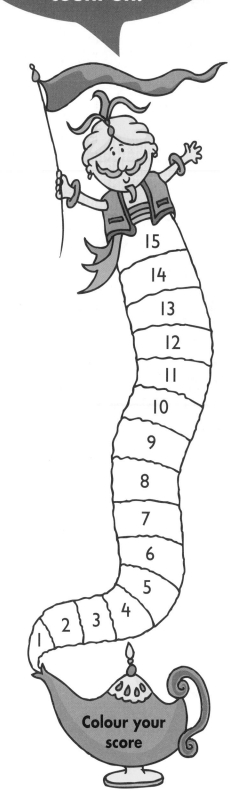

Use the number line. Start with the larger number and count on.

15 14 13 12 11 10 9 8 7 6 5 4 3 2 1

Colour your score

Subtraction

Write the answers.

0 |—|—|—|—|—|—|—|—|—|—|—|—|—|—|—|—|—|—|—|—| 20
           10

Use the number line. Start with the larger number and count back.

1 5 – 3 = ☐

2 6 – 1 = ☐

3 3 – 3 = ☐

4 4 – 1 = ☐

5 6 – 0 = ☐

6 8 – 4 = ☐

7 7 – 7 = ☐

8 6 – 2 = ☐

9 7 – 3 = ☐

10 0 – 0 = ☐

11 9 – 7 = ☐

12 8 – 5 = ☐

13 9 – 3 = ☐

14 7 – 6 = ☐

15 8 – 7 = ☐

Colour your score

14
15
13
12
11
10
9
8
7
6
5
4
3
2
1

Adding ones

Write the answers to the sums.

1 12 + 4 = ☐

2 11 + 5 = ☐

3 10 + 7 = ☐

4 13 + 1 = ☐

5 15 + 3 = ☐

6 14 + 5 = ☐

7 11 + 9 = ☐

8 12 + 7 = ☐

9 17 + 4 = ☐

10 16 + 0 = ☐

11 19 + 5 = ☐

12 14 + 8 = ☐

13 18 + 7 = ☐

14 17 + 6 = ☐

15 16 + 9 = ☐

Add the ones and then the ten.

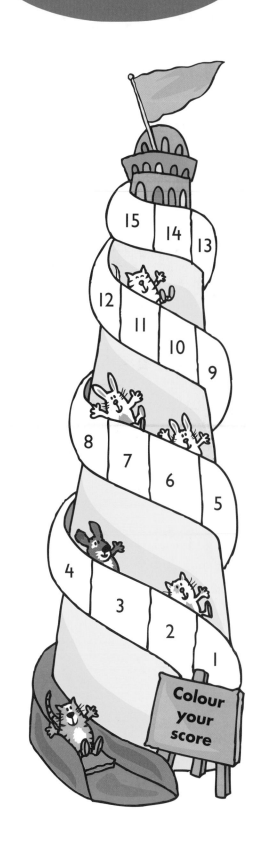

Colour your score

Subtracting ones

Write the answers.

1 16 – 3 = ☐

2 15 – 4 = ☐

3 17 – 1 = ☐

4 18 – 7 = ☐

5 16 – 6 = ☐

6 18 – 0 = ☐

7 14 – 5 = ☐

8 16 – 8 = ☐

9 11 – 7 = ☐

10 12 – 5 = ☐

11 15 – 9 = ☐

12 14 – 8 = ☐

13 17 – 7 = ☐

14 13 – 6 = ☐

15 12 – 9 = ☐

12 – 4 = 8
Start at 12 and
count back 4.
8   9   10   11   12

Colour your score

Addition problems

Write the answers.

1 Tom has 5 comics.
He buys another 6.
How many comics does Tom
have altogether?

[   ] comics

Read each question carefully. Look for the numbers to add on.

2 There are 6 balls in one bag and
8 balls in another bag.
How many balls are there in total?

[   ] balls

3 What is 5 more than 7? [   ]

4 Put together 8 and 5. [   ]

5 Work out the sum of 8 and 3. [   ]

Colour your score

8
7
6
5
4
3
2
1

6 Polly buys 5 red apples and
7 green apples.
How many apples does Polly buy?

[   ] apples

7 What number is 3 greater than 9?

[   ]

8 Sam packs 9 shirts in a suitcase.
He adds another 5 shirts.
How many shirts does Sam pack?

[   ] shirts

Subtraction problems

Write the answers.

1 There are 8 counters on the table.
Obi takes 5 of the counters.
How many counters are left on
the table? ☐ counters

2 Work out 1 less than 5. ☐

3 A pet shop has 5 rabbits.
They sell 5 rabbits.
How many rabbits are left?
☐ rabbits

4 Work out 4 take away 3. ☐

5 Subtract 5 from 7. ☐

6 Nia has 8 buttons on her coat.
2 buttons fall off.
How many buttons are left on
Nia's coat? ☐ buttons

7 The girls ate 12 slices of pizza.
The boys ate 8 slices of pizza.
How many more slices did the girls eat
than the boys? ☐ slices

8 There are 10 children in a group.
6 of the group are girls.
How many boys are in the group?
☐ boys

Write a number sentence for each question to help you.

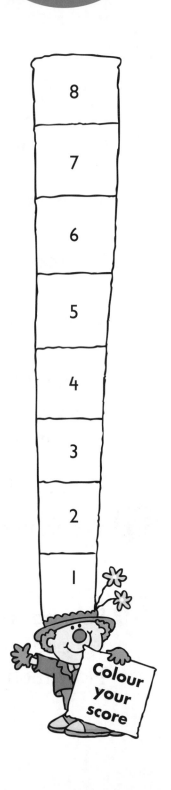

Colour your score

Missing numbers

Fill in the missing numbers.

1. 4 + ☐ = 7

2. 3 + ☐ = 5

3. ☐ + 3 = 8

4. ☐ + 5 = 6

5. ☐ + 7 = 7

6. 4 + ☐ = 11

7. 6 + ☐ = 12

8. 7 + ☐ = 9

9. ☐ + 3 = 12

10. 12 + ☐ = 14

11. ☐ + 8 = 13

12. ☐ + 2 = 17

13. 16 + ☐ = 17

14. ☐ + 7 = 19

15. ☐ + 14 = 18

Try counting on from the given number to the total.

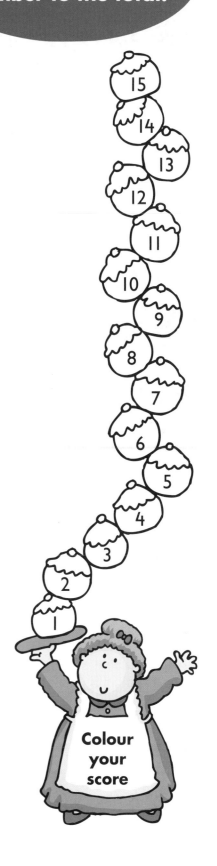

Colour your score

More missing numbers

Fill in the missing numbers.

Try counting back from the larger number to the smaller number.

1   6   –   ☐   =   4

2   3   –   ☐   =   2

3   7   –   ☐   =   5

4   8   –   ☐   =   3

5   9   –   ☐   =   8

6   7   –   ☐   =   0

7   10   –   ☐   =   4

8   12   –   ☐   =   9

9   11   –   ☐   =   5

10   13   –   ☐   =   9

11   18   –   ☐   =   15

12   17   –   ☐   =   9

13   15   –   ☐   =   8

14   13   –   ☐   =   11

15   9   –   ☐   =   0

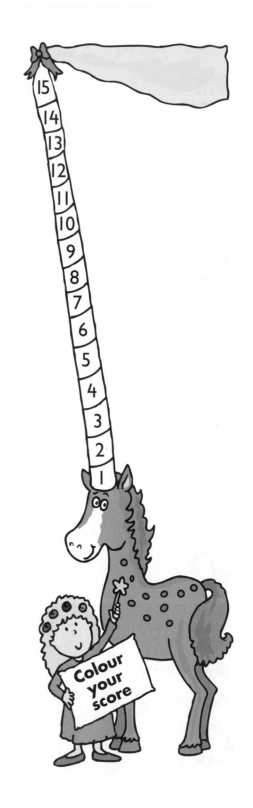

Colour your score

Addition facts to 20

Draw a line to join each sum to the correct total.

Learn these addition facts so you don't have to work them out.

1	3 + 2		8
2	6 + 1		9
3	4 + 2		5
4	5 + 3		7
5	3 + 6		6

6	7 + 1		12
7	5 + 4		8
8	7 + 5		9
9	9 + 4		16
10	8 + 8		13

11	9 + 7		17
12	7 + 7		13
13	8 + 5		15
14	6 + 9		16
15	9 + 8		14

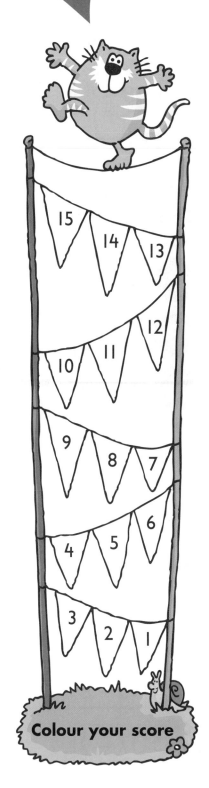

15 14 13
12
10 11
9 8 7
4 5 6
3 2 1

Colour your score

13

Subtraction facts to 20

Draw a line from each subtraction to the correct answer.

Learn these subtraction facts so you don't have to work them out.

1 | 4 – 3

2 | 5 – 2

3 | 6 – 4

4 | 8 – 5

5 | 6 – 5

---

6 | 7 – 2

7 | 8 – 4

8 | 9 – 5

9 | 10 – 4

10 | 11 – 7

---

11 | 13 – 4

12 | 16 – 7

13 | 14 – 6

14 | 15 – 8

15 | 17 – 9

(I)

(2)

(3)

(4)

(5)

(6)

(7)

(8)

(9)

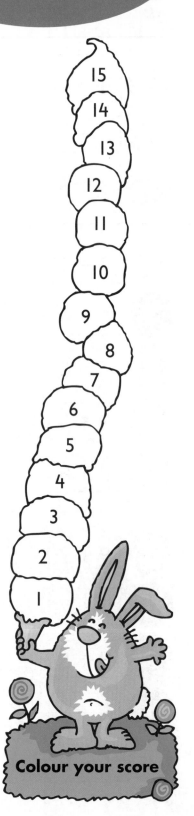

Colour your score

14

Related facts

Fill in the missing numbers.

> The addition and subtraction in each pair use the same numbers.

1 25 + 4 = ☐ and ☐ – 4 = 25

2 31 + 7 = ☐ and ☐ – 7 = 31

3 43 + 6 = ☐ and ☐ – 6 = 43

4 62 + 5 = ☐ and ☐ – 5 = 62

5 21 + 7 = ☐ and ☐ – 7 = 21

6 55 + 3 = ☐ and ☐ – 3 = 55

7 33 + 7 = ☐ and ☐ – 7 = 33

8 85 + 5 = ☐ and ☐ – 5 = 85

9 59 + 3 = ☐ and ☐ – 3 = 59

10 47 + 5 = ☐ and 52 – ☐ = 47

11 62 + 9 = ☐ and 71 – ☐ = 62

12 46 + 8 = ☐ and 54 – ☐ = 46

13 83 + 6 = ☐ and 89 – 6 = ☐

14 54 + 8 = ☐ and 62 – 8 = ☐

15 37 + 9 = ☐ and 46 – 9 = ☐

Colour your score

15

Related facts to 100

Fill in the missing numbers.

Try counting backwards or forwards, or using known number facts.

1 $5 + 3 = $ ☐ , so $50 + 30 = $ ☐

2 $9 - 5 = $ ☐ , so $90 - 50 = $ ☐

3 $2 + 5 = $ ☐ , so $20 + 50 = $ ☐

4 $7 - 4 = $ ☐ , so ☐ $- 40 = 30$

5 $3 + 6 = $ ☐ , so $30 + $ ☐ $= 90$

6 $8 - 4 = $ ☐ , so $80 - 40 = $ ☐

7 $1 + 8 = $ ☐ , so ☐ $+ 80 = 90$

8 $8 - 8 = $ ☐ , so $80 - $ ☐ $= 0$

9 $4 + 5 = $ ☐ , so $40 + 50 = $ ☐

10 $7 - 6 = $ ☐ , so ☐ $- 60 = 10$

11 $1 + 8 = $ ☐ , so $10 + $ ☐ $= 90$

12 $7 - 3 = $ ☐ , so $70 - 30 = $ ☐

13 $4 + 3 = $ ☐ , so ☐ $+ 30 = 70$

14 $10 - 6 = $ ☐ , so $100 - $ ☐ $= 40$

15 $2 + 8 = $ ☐ , so $20 + 80 = $ ☐

Colour your score

Adding tens

Write the answers to these sums.

1. 23 + 10 = ☐
2. 25 + 20 = ☐
3. 39 + 20 = ☐
4. 53 + 10 = ☐
5. 17 + 40 = ☐
6. 32 + 40 = ☐
7. 61 + 20 = ☐
8. 47 + 30 = ☐
9. 26 + 70 = ☐
10. 34 + 50 = ☐
11. 53 + 40 = ☐
12. 85 + 10 = ☐
13. 48 + 40 = ☐
14. 58 + 20 = ☐
15. 87 + 10 = ☐

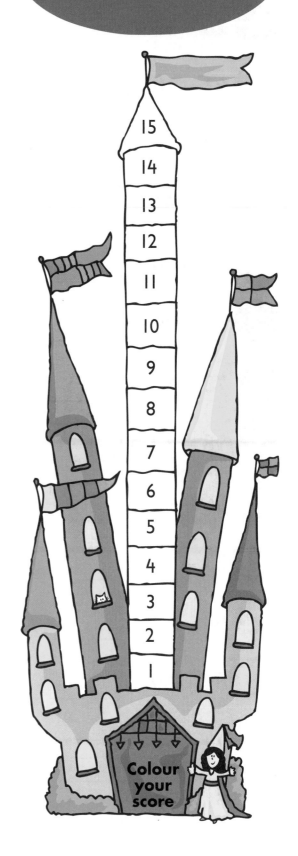

Add the tens. The ones stay the same.

15
14
13
12
11
10
9
8
7
6
5
4
3
2
1

Colour your score

Subtracting tens

Write the answers.

Subtract the tens first. Then write down the ones. The ones stay the same.

1 31 − 10 = ☐

2 26 − 10 = ☐

3 47 − 20 = ☐

4 49 − 30 = ☐

5 63 − 50 = ☐

6 72 − 20 = ☐

7 38 − 30 = ☐

8 78 − 60 = ☐

9 98 − 60 = ☐

10 56 − 40 = ☐

11 83 − 50 = ☐

12 49 − 40 = ☐

13 80 − 60 = ☐

14 74 − 50 = ☐

15 91 − 70 = ☐

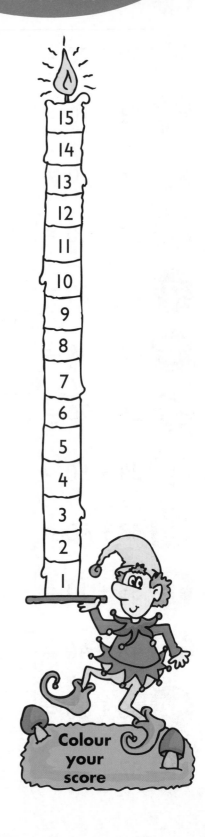

Colour your score

Adding 2-digits

Write the totals.

1 21 + 32 = ☐

2 34 + 23 = ☐

3 16 + 21 = ☐

4 43 + 25 = ☐

5 28 + 51 = ☐

6 35 + 32 = ☐

7 71 + 16 = ☐

8 53 + 33 = ☐

9 62 + 27 = ☐

10 18 + 81 = ☐

11 61 + 36 = ☐

12 57 + 32 = ☐

13 84 + 15 = ☐

14 26 + 53 = ☐

15 53 + 23 = ☐

Use a written method if you need to.

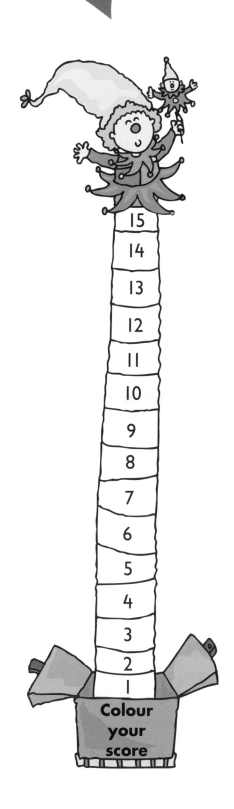

15
14
13
12
11
10
9
8
7
6
5
4
3
2
1
Colour your score

19

Bridging the tens

Write the answers to these sums.

1 28 + 13 =

2 39 + 22 =

3 27 + 25 =

4 34 + 36 =

5 46 + 35 =

6 26 + 57 =

7 78 + 18 =

8 53 + 29 =

9 37 + 58 =

10 47 + 47 =

11 38 + 42 =

12 57 + 18 =

13 59 + 29 =

14 37 + 29 =

15 46 + 38 =

Be careful if the ones add up to 10 or more!

Colour your score

Subtracting 2-digits

Work out the difference between each pair of boxes.

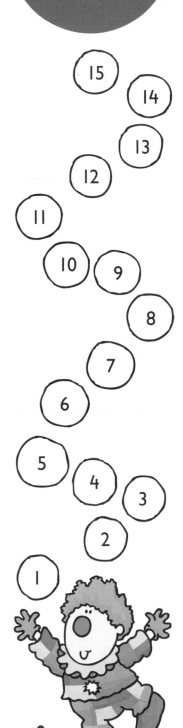

Rewrite the numbers in columns if you need to.

1 46 – 21 = [   ]

2 37 – 15 = [   ]

3 54 – 22 = [   ]

4 48 – 16 = [   ]

5 68 – 25 = [   ]

6 64 – 43 = [   ]

7 59 – 37 = [   ]

8 78 – 28 = [   ]

9 66 – 53 = [   ]

10 94 – 71 = [   ]

11 73 – 22 = [   ]

12 87 – 45 = [   ]

13 75 – 33 = [   ]

14 86 – 53 = [   ]

15 79 – 35 = [   ]

15 14 13 12 11 10 9 8 7 6 5 4 3 2 1

Colour your score

21

More bridging the tens

Write the answers.

1 32 − 18 = [ ]

2 34 − 27 = [ ]

3 45 − 39 = [ ]

4 43 − 26 = [ ]

5 66 − 19 = [ ]

6 57 − 38 = [ ]

7 83 − 25 = [ ]

8 75 − 17 = [ ]

9 62 − 49 = [ ]

10 90 − 63 = [ ]

11 51 − 37 = [ ]

12 92 − 47 = [ ]

13 74 − 37 = [ ]

14 82 − 39 = [ ]

15 73 − 16 = [ ]

Try counting up,
e.g. 33 − 18 = ?

2   10   3

18   20   30   33

2 + 10 + 3 = 15

33 − 18 = 15

Colour your score

Adding three ones

Work out the total number of spots on each group of three ladybirds.

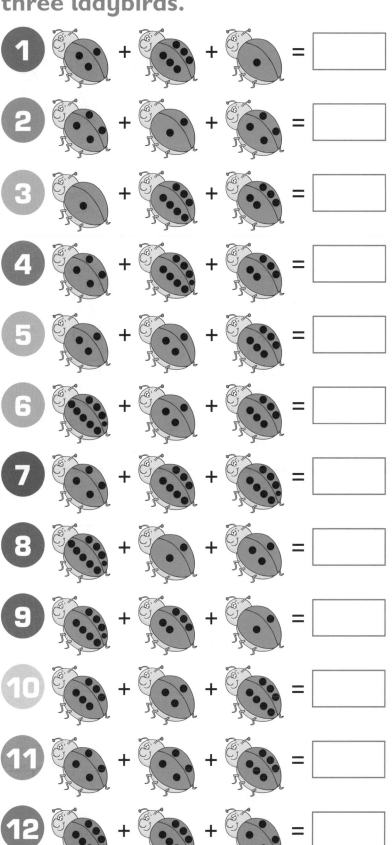

1. [ladybirds] + [ladybirds] + [ladybirds] = ☐
2. [ladybirds] + [ladybirds] + [ladybirds] = ☐
3. [ladybirds] + [ladybirds] + [ladybirds] = ☐
4. [ladybirds] + [ladybirds] + [ladybirds] = ☐
5. [ladybirds] + [ladybirds] + [ladybirds] = ☐
6. [ladybirds] + [ladybirds] + [ladybirds] = ☐
7. [ladybirds] + [ladybirds] + [ladybirds] = ☐
8. [ladybirds] + [ladybirds] + [ladybirds] = ☐
9. [ladybirds] + [ladybirds] + [ladybirds] = ☐
10. [ladybirds] + [ladybirds] + [ladybirds] = ☐
11. [ladybirds] + [ladybirds] + [ladybirds] = ☐
12. [ladybirds] + [ladybirds] + [ladybirds] = ☐

Find two numbers to add first. Use number bonds you know.

12 11 10 9 8 7 6 5 4 3 2 1

Colour your score

23

Partitioning

Fill in the missing numbers.

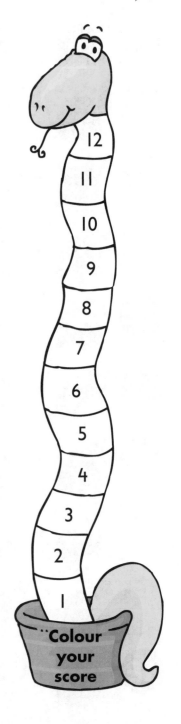

Partition the numbers you are adding or subtracting, e.g. 21 = 20 + 1

1 $21 + 7$
$= 20 + \boxed{} + 7$
$= 28$

7 $36 + 20$
$= 30 + \boxed{} + 6$
$= 56$

2 $36 + 4$
$= \boxed{} + 6 + 4$
$= 40$

8 $25 + 40$
$= \boxed{} + 40 + 5$
$= 65$

3 $58 + 9$
$= 50 + 8 + \boxed{}$
$= 67$

9 $71 + 30$
$= 70 + 30 + \boxed{}$
$= 101$

4 $35 - 2$
$= 30 + 5 - \boxed{}$
$= 33$

10 $47 - 30$
$= 40 - 30 + \boxed{}$
$= 17$

5 $56 - 4$
$= \boxed{} + 6 - 4$
$= 52$

11 $62 - 50$
$= 60 - \boxed{} + 2$
$= 12$

6 $78 - 3$
$= 70 + \boxed{} - 3$
$= 75$

12 $59 - 20$
$= \boxed{} - 20 + 9$
$= 39$

Colour your score

Commutativity

Fill in the missing numbers.

You can add numbers in any order.

1 $6 + 5 = \boxed{} + 6$

2 $9 + 4 = 4 + \boxed{}$

3 $3 + \boxed{} = 6 + 3$

4 $\boxed{} + 3 = 3 + 29$

5 $48 + 8 = 8 + \boxed{}$

6 $71 + 7 = \boxed{} + 71$

7 $64 + \boxed{} = 20 + 64$

8 $\boxed{} + 50 = 50 + 32$

9 $40 + 3 = 3 + \boxed{}$

10 $32 + 47 = \boxed{} + 32$

11 $54 + \boxed{} = 17 + 54$

12 $\boxed{} + 34 = 34 + 43$

13 $5 + 8 + 5 = \boxed{} + 5 + 8$

14 $9 + 7 + 9 = 9 + \boxed{} + 7$

15 $2 + 5 + 8 = \boxed{} + 2 + 5$

Colour your score

25

Families of four

Use each set of three numbers to complete the four number sentences.

1 2, 5, 7

2 + 5 = ☐

5 + 2 = ☐

7 − 5 = ☐

7 − 2 = ☐

5 3, 7, 10

☐ + ☐ = ☐

☐ + ☐ = ☐

☐ − ☐ = ☐

☐ − ☐ = ☐

The subtractions will start with the largest number.

2 1, 4, 5

☐ + ☐ = ☐

☐ + ☐ = ☐

☐ − ☐ = ☐

☐ − ☐ = ☐

6 4, 5, 9

☐ + ☐ = ☐

☐ + ☐ = ☐

☐ − ☐ = ☐

☐ − ☐ = ☐

3 3, 5, 8

☐ + ☐ = ☐

☐ + ☐ = ☐

☐ − ☐ = ☐

☐ − ☐ = ☐

7 5, 6, 11

☐ + ☐ = ☐

☐ + ☐ = ☐

☐ − ☐ = ☐

☐ − ☐ = ☐

4 4, 6, 10

☐ + ☐ = ☐

☐ + ☐ = ☐

☐ − ☐ = ☐

☐ − ☐ = ☐

8 7, 8, 15

☐ + ☐ = ☐

☐ + ☐ = ☐

☐ − ☐ = ☐

☐ − ☐ = ☐

Colour your score

Using the inverse

Write the inverse calculation to check the sum.

Use a tick or cross to show if the sum is correct or wrong.

1 34 + 18 = 52 ☐ _____

2 43 + 21 = 63 ☐ _____

3 56 + 28 = 74 ☐ _____

4 64 + 32 = 96 ☐ _____

5 20 + 56 = 76 ☐ _____

6 54 + 36 = 80 ☐ _____

7 38 + 34 = 72 ☐ _____

8 57 + 28 = 85 ☐ _____

9 73 + 19 = 91 ☐ _____

10 28 + 38 = 56 ☐ _____

11 27 + 43 = 70 ☐ _____

12 37 + 47 = 84 ☐ _____

13 52 + 27 = 79 ☐ _____

14 48 + 42 = 90 ☐ _____

15 37 + 45 = 84 ☐ _____

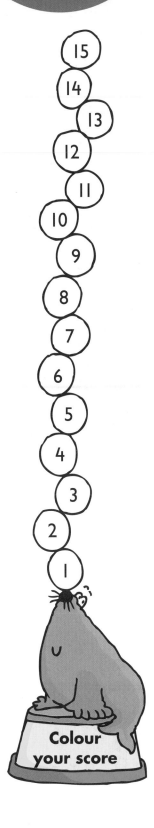

15
14
13
12
11
10
9
8
7
6
5
4
3
2
1

Colour your score

More using the inverse

Write the inverse calculation to check the subtraction.

Use a tick or cross to show if the subtraction is correct or wrong.

Start with the answer and add the subtracted number.

1 $31 - 11 = 20$ ☐ _____

2 $46 - 24 = 22$ ☐ _____

3 $41 - 18 = 37$ ☐ _____

4 $54 - 29 = 25$ ☐ _____

5 $51 - 26 = 35$ ☐ _____

6 $60 - 26 = 44$ ☐ _____

7 $73 - 55 = 22$ ☐ _____

8 $57 - 25 = 32$ ☐ _____

9 $81 - 26 = 55$ ☐ _____

10 $78 - 34 = 44$ ☐ _____

11 $68 - 29 = 39$ ☐ _____

12 $42 - 16 = 26$ ☐ _____

13 $74 - 27 = 47$ ☐ _____

14 $68 - 29 = 41$ ☐ _____

15 $54 - 38 = 26$ ☐ _____

Colour your score

15
14
13
12
11
10
9
8
7
6
5
4
3
2
1

Find the numbers

Fill in the missing numbers.

1 34 + [ ] = 52

2 21 + [ ] = 48

3 47 + [ ] = 61

4 27 + [ ] = 42

5 [ ] + 32 = 70

6 [ ] + 51 = 78

7 [ ] + 16 = 64

8 43 + [ ] = 72

9 [ ] + 32 = 54

10 [ ] + 42 = 80

11 63 + [ ] = 85

12 [ ] + 44 = 67

13 [ ] + 35 = 71

14 73 + [ ] = 94

15 14 + [ ] = 61

Use the inverse. Subtract to find the missing number.

15
14
13
12
11
10
9
8
7
6
5
4
3
2
1

Colour your score

29

More find the numbers

Fill in the missing numbers.

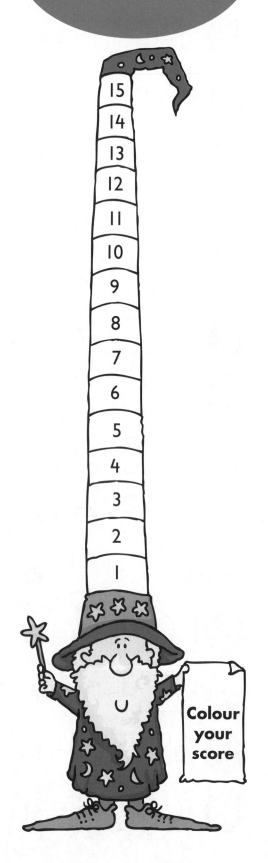

Decide whether to add or subtract the numbers.

1 56 – ☐ = 36

2 ☐ – 43 = 12

3 51 – ☐ = 28

4 ☐ – 22 = 43

5 82 – ☐ = 68

6 ☐ – 14 = 39

7 75 – ☐ = 27

8 ☐ – 63 = 17

9 31 – ☐ = 18

10 ☐ – 15 = 67

11 68 – ☐ = 43

12 ☐ – 19 = 29

13 74 – ☐ = 36

14 ☐ – 51 = 24

15 73 – ☐ = 58

Colour your score

Word problems

Write the answers.

Read each question carefully to decide whether to add or subtract.

1 Add 26 and 28. ☐

2 There are 24 red counters and 35 blue counters in a jar. How many counters are there altogether? ☐ counters

3 A bus has 26 seats downstairs and 38 seats upstairs. How many seats are there in total on the bus? ☐ seats

4 Put together 37 and 35. ☐

5 Mandeep collects 80 cards. She gives 12 to a friend. How many does Mandeep have left? ☐ cards

6 Work out the difference between 26 and 85. ☐

7 There are 100 stickers in a set. Ben has 45 stickers. How many more stickers does Ben need for a set? ☐ stickers

8 A farmer collects 47 eggs on Saturday and 38 eggs on Sunday. How many eggs does he collect altogether? ☐ eggs

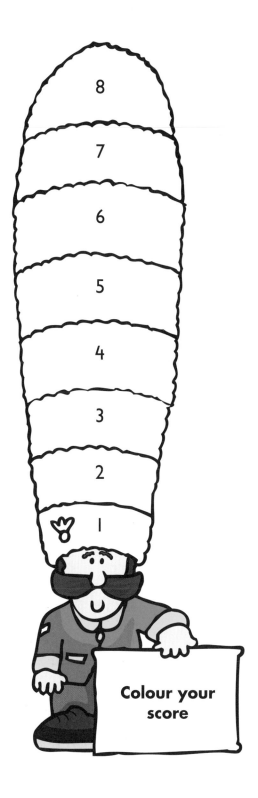

Colour your score

8
7
6
5
4
3
2
1

Answers

Counting on
1. 5
2. 8
3. 7
4. 8
5. 8
6. 6
7. 10
8. 9
9. 13
10. 10

Taking away
1. 4
2. 2
3. 3
4. 3
5. 6
6. 5
7. 0
8. 7
9. 1
10. 6

Number facts to 20
1. 4
2. 3
3. 5
4. 5
5. 7
6. 2
7. 8
8. 8
9. 15
10. 7

Addition
1. 7
2. 6
3. 6
4. 9
5. 6
6. 11
7. 11
8. 12
9. 10
10. 14
11. 14
12. 10
13. 9
14. 17
15. 14

Subtraction
1. 2
2. 5
3. 0
4. 3
5. 6
6. 4
7. 0
8. 4
9. 4
10. 0
11. 2
12. 3
13. 6
14. 1
15. 1

Adding ones
1. 16
2. 16
3. 17
4. 14
5. 18
6. 19
7. 20
8. 19
9. 21
10. 16
11. 24
12. 22
13. 25
14. 23
15. 25

Subtracting ones
1. 13
2. 11
3. 16
4. 11
5. 10
6. 18
7. 9
8. 8
9. 4
10. 7
11. 6
12. 6
13. 10
14. 7
15. 3

Addition problems
1. 11 comics
2. 14 balls
3. 12
4. 13
5. 11
6. 12 apples
7. 12
8. 14 shirts

Subtraction problems
1. 3 counters
2. 4
3. 0 rabbits
4. 1
5. 2
6. 6 buttons
7. 4 slices
8. 4 boys

Missing numbers
1. 3
2. 2
3. 5
4. 1
5. 0
6. 7
7. 6
8. 2
9. 9
10. 2
11. 5
12. 15
13. 1
14. 12
15. 4

More missing numbers
1. 2
2. 1
3. 2
4. 5
5. 1
6. 7
7. 6
8. 3
9. 6
10. 4
11. 3
12. 8
13. 7
14. 2
15. 9

Addition facts to 20
1. 5
2. 7
3. 6
4. 8
5. 9
6. 8
7. 9
8. 12
9. 13
10. 16
11. 16
12. 14
13. 13
14. 15
15. 17

Subtraction facts to 20
1. 1
2. 3
3. 2
4. 3
5. 1
6. 5
7. 4
8. 4
9. 6
10. 4
11. 9
12. 9
13. 8
14. 7
15. 8

Related facts
1. 29, 29
2. 38, 38
3. 49, 49
4. 67, 67
5. 28, 28
6. 58, 58
7. 40, 40
8. 90, 90
9. 62, 62
10. 52, 5
11. 71, 9
12. 54, 8
13. 89, 83
14. 62, 54
15. 46, 37

Related facts to 100
1. 8, 80
2. 4, 40
3. 7, 70
4. 3, 70
5. 9, 60
6. 4, 40
7. 9, 10
8. 0, 80
9. 9, 90
10. 1, 70
11. 9, 80
12. 4, 40
13. 7, 40
14. 4, 60
15. 10, 100

Adding tens
1. 33
2. 45
3. 59
4. 63
5. 57
6. 72
7. 81
8. 77
9. 96
10. 84
11. 93
12. 95
13. 88
14. 78
15. 97

Subtracting tens
1. 21
2. 16
3. 27
4. 19
5. 13
6. 52
7. 8
8. 18
9. 38
10. 16
11. 33
12. 9
13. 20
14. 24
15. 21

Adding 2-digits
1. 53
2. 57
3. 37
4. 68
5. 79
6. 67
7. 87
8. 86
9. 89
10. 99
11. 97
12. 89
13. 99
14. 79
15. 76